HEAVEN SPEAKS ABOUT STRESS

Direction for Our Times
As given to Anne, a lay apostle

Heaven Speaks About Stress

Direction for Our Times
As given to Anne, a lay apostle

ISBN: 978-1-933684-02-4

© Copyright 2005-2013 Direction for Our Times. All rights reserved. No part of this book may be used or reproduced in any manner whatsoever without written permission.

Publisher:
Direction for Our Times
9000 West 81st Street
Justice, IL 60458
708-496-9300
contactus@directionforourtimes.org

www.directionforourtimes.org

Direction for Our Times is a 501(c)(3) tax-exempt organization.

Manufactured in the United States of America

V0313

Direction for Our Times wishes to manifest its complete obedience and submission of mind and heart to the final and definitive judgment of the Magisterium of the Catholic Church and the local Ordinary regarding the supernatural character of the messages received by Anne, a lay apostle.

In this spirit, the messages of Anne, a lay apostle, have been submitted to her bishop, Most Reverend Leo O'Reilly, Bishop of Kilmore, Ireland, and to the Vatican Congregation for the Doctrine of the Faith for formal examination. In the meantime Bishop O'Reilly has given permission for their publication.

Table of Contents

August 9, 2005

    Jesus 1
    St. Padre Pio 3
    St. Padre Pio 5
    St. Padre Pio 7
    St. Padre Pio 9
    St. Padre Pio 11
    Blessed Mother 13

August 9, 2005
Jesus

My children, why do you hurry so? Why do you feel you must move so quickly through your days? This is not the way I intended the children of God to live. You may tell Me that you have many things to do. I respond to you by saying that you are trying to do too much. You will not be holy if you move so quickly. I want My beloved apostles to move more slowly and thoughtfully through their days. I want you to make decisions on what I am asking you to do and what you are busying yourself with that is not from Me. I want your way of life to change and I am asking you to make this change now. In the next week, think about each activity and decide, with Me, if it is something I want you to do or something you want to do. My dearest apostles, I ask that you begin to remove activities that do not further My will. I want more time in silence, as you know. I want more time with families, without noise blocking you from each other. I want prayer, yes, but also conversations that are not hurried and stressed between husbands and wives, brothers and sisters, and parents and children. These are the souls I have decided you will walk through your life with and you have obligations to them. If you are too busy with your own will, you are not seeing to Mine and you are missing opportunities both to learn from others and to assist others in learning about Me. If you do not pay heed to Me, who will? In order for the renewal to come, My beloved apostles must begin to seek only heaven's will in their days. And I am talking to you and calling you My apostle. Do not look to someone else or assume I am speaking to others. I am speaking to you.

St. Padre Pio

Live simply. Eat simply. Love one another simply. Do not complicate matters unnecessarily. How do you live simply? You remove activities that are not necessary or that pull you away from duty. Consider your duty. Then move through each day and try to serve only that duty. Have order in your life and in the life of your family. There should be a rhythm to each day that does not change. Rise at the same time. Retire at the same time in the evening. Pray at the same time. This creates an environment in which you are free to consider God. Do not think, my friends, that you live in a world where the need for simplicity has disappeared. Apostles of Jesus Christ must set an example of service and obedience but not hectic service. There should be calm and if there is not calm in your life, change your life and keep changing it until you find calm. The act of sitting and reading these words is forcing you to consider heaven's wishes for you. Pull yourself away from the world even further and spend some time in silence when you are finished with reading. Ask Jesus to show you which activities should be removed. My friends, the lives of your children, if you are a parent, should also be simple. Children should not be stressed by too many activities. They should have responsibilities in their home and their parents should be present to see that the children meet their responsibilities. This will make children feel good and holy. If there is calm in the home, and not constant noise, a parent is able to consider each child and see that each child is proceeding in the acquisition of virtues. This is not happening if there is a constant stream of activity that prevents souls from consideration of these matters. Live simply.

St. Padre Pio

Eat simply. There is a problem with eating and drinking in today's world. There are those who are starving and those who are gorging. My friends, I loved food when I lived on earth. I loved it so much that I had to withdraw from it lest I became too attached to it. Food is for sustenance. You should eat simple foods, prepared at home, and not stress your body with too much food or too much drink. This is not how holy apostles live. Holy apostles consider what they need to sustain their bodies so they can serve each other in physical strength. There is a time for feasting, of course, and these feasts should be as generous as possible with great thanksgiving and joy. I am not saying that there should be no joy or that food should be dreary. Mealtime should be happy and cheerful. There should be prayers before meals and after meals. These prayers should not be long or drawn out. They should be simple and heartfelt, thanking heaven for providing for you on each day. What I am remarking upon is a distorted view of food and eating. If you are part of a family, there should be others assisting in the preparation and serving of meals. Even if there is limited time, there should be some form of sitting together and ministering to one another with regard to each day's challenges or triumphs. If you are eating alone, this time of eating can be shared with heaven. It is heaven who is sustaining you, after all, so it is only just that heaven be given some attention. Eating should create a pause in your day. It is a time for reflection, a break between one task and the next, between one portion of your day and another. It is a time to consider your duty and how you are doing in the performance of it. Eating in haste is yet another example of how the enemy keeps God's children so distracted that they cannot consider Him or His will. Eat simply.

St. Padre Pio

Love simply. Serve each other in joy and patience. There is far too much talk about relationships. You were created to serve, dear apostles. Serve. Do not keep scorecards of who is serving the most or who is serving the best. You have only to account for yourself, so why do you concern yourself so often with the lack of service in others? Set an example of consistent service and you will find that others fall into line with you and improve. Love each other as Jesus loves you. Jesus forgives and forgets. Jesus does not wait to catch you at a bad moment when you are not doing your best or when you are discouraged. Jesus encourages you and overlooks your flaws. Do this for others, most particularly the souls who are called to walk through your life with you. No judging, my friends. Judging is for Jesus. Put the best possible light on others and expect the best from them and you will not be disappointed. Love passionately in that if you are called to walk with someone, be loyal to him as Jesus is loyal to you. Look for ways to make him feel cherished and appreciated. Small acts of kindness can change someone's life. Heaven is promising the greatest graces for this time. Heaven speaks the truth, always, and will deliver these graces. Ask for great graces for each soul in your life, particularly that soul who is annoying to you or the soul you feel is failing you in some way. Ask heaven to surround him with grace and then love him. Dear parents, love your children simply. Look at each child as God's precious gift, created to serve the Kingdom. How will that soul be called to serve? Each call is individual but I can tell you this. If there is a child in your life, you must consider what you are being asked to contribute to that child's formation. I am speaking now to all people, not just parents. Take an interest in the children around you and see what our Lord is expecting you to provide in the way of encouragement. Brothers and sisters, serve each other in peace and do not fight and bicker so much. Love simply. Heaven will help you.

St. Padre Pio

Be at peace in the crosses God has asked you to carry. Do not be angry at heaven or blame heaven for the troubles in your life. Your life will end and the troubles will end. If you are at odds with heaven, your anger is misplaced. Brothers and sisters, neither should there be so much energy scrutinizing what your Church has done wrong. Acknowledge the mistakes of others, and pray for them. Protect yourself from their flaws if they are dangerous to you, but do not live your life discussing the flaws and mistakes of those in the Church who are struggling. This is over. The time for this has passed. A renewed Church is coming, faithful and united, and you must help to usher this in by setting an example of great loyalty and fidelity. Perhaps there are things you do not agree with about this Church. Heaven accepts the fact that you have opinions. But you should discuss these things with Jesus and not use these points to pull your Church down and distance others from obedience. You will be accountable for this, my friends. If Jesus is calling you to lead in the Church, then you must lead. If He is calling you to follow in the Church, I suggest you follow or risk displeasing heaven. These words I say to you are serious and I am praying that you will heed them. God is allowing this because He loves you and He does not want you confused and distracted. This relentless criticism of the Church is not from God, of course. But you know that and you understand that being in a constant state of disagreement with your Church is causing you unnecessary stress. There are many beautiful and brave souls who have been called to the renewal. You are one of them. Work for your Church and defend Her in whatever way you are called. This is God's one true Church and that has not changed. Be faithful during this time and your reward will fill you with the greatest joy. It is too uncomfortable for you to be doubtful of our Lord's leaders. So you should be accepting of both your personal crosses and also accepting of the crosses your Church is carrying during this period. Heaven is with you in each personal cross and heaven is working to renew the Church. Be patient and calm while we work together in these matters.

St. Padre Pio

My brothers and sisters have many ways of dealing with stress in their lives. What heaven is trying to tell you is that much of your stress can be alleviated by a few simple decisions. The first is a decision for Jesus, total and complete. This will actually reduce all of the stress in your life because you will begin to live for heaven and not earth. You will concentrate on your duty, ordained by heaven, and not on the busyness that the world is trying to substitute for your duty. You will decide to live simply, eat simply, love simply, and heaven will surround you with graces each day. Jesus will not be in one box and your life in another. Jesus and your life will be together each day, all day, and each decision will be made in union with Him. This is service to heaven and unity with heaven. Concentrate not on how others are loving you or not loving you. Jesus loves you enough for everyone on the planet with you at any given time. Concentrate on how Jesus is able to flow His love through you to others. This is the renewal. This is the process of the Second Coming which has begun. Jesus returns to the earth through each one of His beloved apostles. If you are thinking that perhaps you are not called to be His apostle, let me clear that up immediately and state, with all certainty, that Jesus is calling you. You are called. You must answer. Follow Him and you will find your stress fading away, even in the greatest of trials and temptations. I am your friend and heaven is filled with souls like me who are also your friends. We will help you with the process of reducing stress in your life. Acquire a heavenly rhythm to your days and watch what Jesus can do. I love you.

Blessed Mother

My little children become unhappy when they are too busy. They do not have time to give love to each other and to receive love from each other and this makes them troubled. They then seek to make themselves feel better by distractions that are not from God. Dear children, I am your heavenly mother and I will help you with this problem. Jesus wants you to live happily, even with the inevitable crosses that come in your lifetime. Be aware of each act that pulls you away from your duty. Be disciplined in organizing your life so that there is order and peace in your home. Do not allow possessions to clutter your home or your heart. Remove these material things and let your home be clean and orderly, as best you can. I am not asking that you be rigid, my dear children, but that you be simple. I am not asking that you be harsh with your children but that you set an example of order so that they will understand that too many possessions are not necessary. I will help you to be at peace with each other in your home. Please do not shout at each other. When this happens, and impatience takes over, apologize as quickly as possible and restore peace. Do not live in coldness. If there is a disagreement and you make peace, even if you are not at fault, all of heaven will applaud you. Blessed are the peacemakers, my children. This cannot be stated enough. Bring peace everywhere with you and you will be a faithful apostle of my beautiful Son, Jesus. I am with you and I will help you to understand how heaven is asking you to do this. Always look for the small opportunities. I love you. I will never leave you.

Lay Apostles of Jesus Christ the Returning King

We seek to be united to Jesus in our daily work, and through our vocations, in order to obtain graces for the conversion of sinners. We pledge our allegiance to God the Father. Through our cooperation with the Holy Spirit, we will allow Jesus to flow through us into the world, bringing His light. We do this in union with Mary, our Blessed Mother, with the Communion of Saints, with all of God's holy angels, and with our fellow lay apostles in the world.

As lay apostles of Jesus Christ the Returning King, we agree to adopt the following spiritual practices, as best we can.

1. Allegiance Prayer, along with the Morning Offering and a brief prayer for the Holy Father.

2. One hour of Eucharistic Adoration each week.

3. Participation in a monthly lay apostle prayer group, which includes the Luminous Mysteries of the Holy Rosary, and the reading of the Monthly Message.

4. Monthly Confession.

5. Further, we will follow the example of Jesus Christ as set out in Holy Scripture, treating all others with His patience and kindness.

Promise from Jesus to His Lay Apostles:

May 12, 2005

Your message to souls remains constant. Welcome each soul to the rescue mission. You may assure each lay apostle that just as they concern themselves with My interests, I will concern Myself with theirs. They will be placed in My Sacred Heart and I will defend and protect them. I will also pursue complete conversion of each of their loved ones. So you see, the souls who serve in this rescue mission as My beloved lay apostles will know peace. The world cannot make this promise, as only heaven can bestow peace on a soul. This is truly heaven's mission and I call every one of heaven's children to assist Me. You will be well rewarded, My dear ones.

Allegiance Prayer

Dear God in heaven, I pledge my allegiance to You. I give You my life, my work, and my heart. In turn, give me the grace of obeying Your every direction to the fullest possible extent. Amen.

Morning Offering

O Jesus, through the Immaculate Heart of Mary, I offer You the prayers, works, joys, and sufferings of this day, for all the intentions of Your Sacred Heart, in union with the Holy Sacrifice of the Mass throughout the world, in reparation for my sins, and for the intentions of the Holy Father. Amen.

Five Luminous Mysteries:

1. The Baptism of Jesus
2. The Wedding at Cana
3. The Proclamation of the Kingdom of God
4. The Transfiguration
5. The Institution of the Eucharist

The Volumes

*Direction for Our Times
as given to Anne, a lay apostle*

Volume One:	***Thoughts on Spirituality***
Volume Two:	***Conversations with the Eucharistic Heart of Jesus***
Volume Three:	***God the Father Speaks to His Children*** ***The Blessed Mother Speaks to Her Bishops and Priests***
Volume Four:	***Jesus the King*** ***Heaven Speaks to Priests*** ***Jesus Speaks to Sinners***
Volume Six:	***Heaven Speaks to Families***
Volume Seven:	***Greetings from Heaven***
Volume Nine:	***Angels***
Volume Ten:	***Jesus Speaks to His Apostles***

Volumes Five and Eight will be printed at a later date.

The Volumes are now available in PDF format for free download and printing from our website:
www.directionforourtimes.org.
We encourage everyone to print and distribute them.

The Volumes are also available at your local bookstore.

The "Heaven Speaks" Booklets

*Direction for Our Times
as given to Anne, a lay apostle*

The following booklets are available individually from Direction for Our Times:

Heaven Speaks About Abortion
Heaven Speaks About Addictions
Heaven Speaks to Victims of Clerical Abuse
Heaven Speaks to Consecrated Souls
Heaven Speaks About Depression
Heaven Speaks About Divorce
Heaven Speaks to Prisoners
Heaven Speaks to Soldiers
Heaven Speaks About Stress
Heaven Speaks to Young Adults

Heaven Speaks to Those Away from the Church
Heaven Speaks to Those Considering Suicide
Heaven Speaks to Those Who Do Not Know Jesus
Heaven Speaks to Those Who Are Dying
Heaven Speaks to Those Who Experience Tragedy
Heaven Speaks to Those Who Fear Purgatory
Heaven Speaks to Those Who Have Rejected God
Heaven Speaks to Those Who Struggle to Forgive
Heaven Speaks to Those Who Suffer from Financial Need
Heaven Speaks to Parents Who Worry About Their Children's Salvation

All twenty of the "Heaven Speaks" booklets are now available in PDF format for free download and printing from our website www.directionforourtimes.org. We encourage everyone to print and distribute these booklets.

This book is part of a non-profit mission.
Our Lord has requested that we
spread these words internationally.

Please help us.

If you would like to participate,
please contact us at:

Direction for Our Times
9000 West 81st Street
Justice, Illinois 60458

708-496-9300
contactus@directionforourtimes.org
www.directionforourtimes.org

Direction for Our Times Ireland
The Hague Building
Cullies
Cavan
County Cavan
Ireland

Phone: 353-(0)49-437-3040
Email: contactus@dfot.ie

Jesus gives Anne a message for the
world on the first day of each month.
To receive the monthly messages
you may access our website at
www.directionforourtimes.org
or call us at 708-496-9300
to be placed on our mailing list.